Captivity Narrative

WINNER OF THE 1999

OHIO STATE UNIVERSITY PRESS /

THE JOURNAL AWARD IN POETRY

Captivity Narrative

Mary Ann Samyn

OHIO STATE UNIVERSITY PRESS

COLUMBUS

Library of Congress Cataloging-in-Publication Data

Samyn, Mary Ann, 1970–
    Captivity narrative / Mary Ann Samyn.
       p.   cm.
    "Winner of the 1997 Ohio State University Press / The journal award
in poetry."
    Includes bibliographical references (p.   )
    ISBN 0-8142-0832-0 (cloth : alk. paper). — ISBN 0-8142-5034-3
(paper : alk. paper)
    1. Captivity Poetry.   2. Women Poetry.   I. Title.
PS3569.A46695C37   1999
811'.54—dc21
                                             99-24695
                                                CIP

Text and jacket design by Diane Gleba Hall.
Type set in Perpetua by G & S Typesetters, Inc.
Printed by Sheridan Books.

9 8 7 6 5 4 3 2 1

Acknowledgments

Grateful acknowledgment is made to the editors of the publications in which the following poems first appeared:

The Bitter Oleander: "The Parts of a Flower"

Controlled Burn: "The Sorceress"

Denver Quarterly: "Devilkin"

The Kenyon Review: "A Short History of Anxiety"

Field: "Gretel: A Case Study" and "Interview with Alice"

The Journal: "Enough" and "Mockingbird Pie"

The Laurel Review: "The Disappearing Girl," "The Disappearing Girl Explains," "The Disappearing Girl's Mother Remembers," "Her Sisters Agree," "His Bag of Tricks," and "The Magician Explains How"

Many Mountains Moving: "After Arguing"

The Montserrat Review: "Alice Falling," "Cracked Alice," and "Thoroughly Modern Alice"

no røses review: "The Bitter End," "One Thing or Another," and "Reality Trick"

Northwest Review: "The Mesmerist"

The Ohio Review: "Lake Bottom" and "Planetarium"

Poem: "The Bereavement Room"

Poet Lore: "Alice Writes Her Memoirs"

Readings from the Midwest Poetry Festival: "Trompe l'Oeil in Winter"

Small Pond: "Alice in the Hallway"

Verse: "The Listening Room"

The Virginia Quarterly Review: "Bright Waiting" and "Devil and the Deep Blue Sea"

Many thanks to my teachers and friends in the creative writing program at the University of Virginia: Rita Dove, Greg Orr, Lisa Russ Spaar, and especially Charles Wright; to Ed Hoeppner; and to Sue Varady, who stayed with me.

*for my mother and father
for my sister Ellen
and for Gerry (who knew——)*

Contents

A Note about the Book

The structure of this book, as the title indicates, is based on early American "captivity narratives," accounts of frontier captures, which were divided not into sections or chapters but into "removes" that indicated a change in location from one wilderness encampment to another.

Captivity narratives are especially important in the history of women's literature, and Mary Rowlandson's account was the first full-length prose work published by an American woman. Excerpts from both *The Narrative of the Captivity and Restoration of Mrs. Mary Rowlandson* and *A Narrative of the Life of Mrs. Mary Jemison* appear as italicized portions of the removes in this book.

Finally, although most of these stories conclude with the return to "civilization," "rescues" were not always as welcome as one might imagine. Early editions of captivity narratives edited out such ambivalence, however, replacing it with religious instruction about God's providence and the deliverance from wilderness. Yet, like many stories, the narratives themselves continue to question the nature and location (interior or exterior, for example) of that wilderness and what it means to be lost, or found.

*Their glittering weapons so daunted my spirit,
that I chose rather to go along.*

—*Mary Rowlandson*

First Remove

The gray, the blank,
the sky above my head.

Gather it in:
pocket pocket.

Acorns drop and split.
Am I to take the blame?

Quick! to the door:
bar and cower.

(A ripple, a nothing. What *besets my house,* my small frame? I hang
the wash in no particular wind. I think of supper: my knife and
fork, my clean plate. If there are animals lurking, I do not hear
them. I do not know their names.)

Reality Trick

Keep is the room I know
too well: noise of settling,
birds in the eaves.

Lock of evening,
I'm down on my knees.
My voice pleads and shreds.

A black lake at each wrist,
wind carries off my arms,
these twigs that beg.

Boundlessness then:
a creak, a hinge.
And stealth, I slip

from hive and buzz,
to *hush!* the thrill
and quiet after.

Lessons in the Invisible

Not flame but
red in the trees and burning,
the sound of my hands in grief.
My face

clouds, small bones
loosening into whispers:
impossible flight, keyholes.
Then this

horizon
where I've stood, what's vertical,
my pale body slipping through
black, cold.

The arrow
taut in my back flies toward night,
my once round mouth an echo,
hardened.

Trompe l'Oeil in Winter

Everything white, the lake's cheek, turns
whiter, birds like hands at its sad mouth.

Snow at the edges, my body, trees' black
pale into blank landscape, then less, a vanishing

text gone like my name in breath against
the glass, the window flown off, its shuttered

wings beating. For mirrors now, only ice,
a tongueless mouth, entire alphabets swallowed,

the verb for dusk, the cold and foreign sky.
Shadows kneel in the dark boat of night,

its thick voice like deep rowing overhead,
beyond the moon and past the frigid stars.

Lake Bottom

Surely someone pouts there:
the owner of the hand

struggling among the cattails,
what we call *wind,*

a chill rising. In shallows
now, as though the tumbling —

bridge rail, dark shot down —
did not occur or could lead

to recovery. As though
a stray shoe — high heel —

could elicit something more
than fright at how close

the air's become, how tangled
the grasses that rush the shore.

The Listening Room

i

Snap and gleam, buck teeth,
the white picket fence, eager

as always and vines, vines,
sticky blossoms, coy and pawing.

Is this my hand? Am I the reason
for the garden gate, neglected,

inconsolable on its hinge?
A rustle, the grass shifts and opens:

flagstones dull as mirrors draped
in mourning. Now a path, a door,

the curtain moved aside, and me,
barely standing in my mother's heels.

ii

Inside the doorbell, sudden cheer:
these Russian dolls nested one

inside another, their red and blue
aprons fringed in white, ready

for work or dancing. Armless
and coiled in weeds grown loud

as bracelets, the house a wrist
and vulnerable, the dolls chime

in, lips barely parted, wooden
teeth whistling. At the slightest

touch, they quicken and spill,
desperate for the curve of my hand.

iii

This must be where I left
my Sunday shoes, my reflection

in black patent leather, thin
straps and buckles gleaming.

Inside, a puppet theater where
everything hollow once spoke

in my voice, even the mirror
I broke, the scolding and bad luck.

Is this the nursery where I slept?
Is this the bed with the bars?

Sheep dangled from the ceiling.
Shorn and cold, they bleated

all night. Who tended their cuts?
What became of their fleecy coats?

Even the dolls' cracked faces
cried for attention, their fingertips

chipped and pleading.
Who would want more of this?

The train I wished for
rushes inside the wall, rattles

the dishes, unnerves the teacups.
Dust calculates what has passed;

the calendar curls on its nail.
Old habit, weather report,

I lift a glass to the door: a clock,
its ticking, or small gasps?

iv

The hush and spotlight, three rings,
my mother in the tall hat.
Black and ribboned, she towers.

Inside it, she keeps three oranges
to lure me, a pair of angora mittens,
my favorite hairbrush.

Beneath my coat, each sequin
she stitched dangles on its thread.
I am cold, unraveling.

She claps her arthritic hands.
So pleased to see me, she offers
any trick: the highwire and bicycle,

the polished teeth of her best lions.
My pancake makeup cracks.
She promises darkness and ovations.

Pink-feathered and jingling,
the trick pony nods his head,
stamps his foot in the dirt.

v

All this impatience, and my ticking
watch. Inside it, a forest and dolls
whose mouths move like mine:

primitive language, darkness
off my lips. Bees provide the pulse,
that green and brooding vine.

Once, a crescent moon tucked
inside the sky: a lock of hair clipped
for fear or memory, disguised as luck:

a coin hidden up my sleeve:
a train on the tracks, the whistle
singing through my hollow wrists.

vi
The music starts, then galloping:
the painted horses' wild mouths

and eyes, the sweep and circle,
a carousel at night, lights pulsing

through the yard. Cotton candy
flames in my hand, my mother

a blur as I go by, my body tight
to the one I chose for its magic

saddle of fading constellations,
its dark legs, its fierce and eager grin.

Second Remove

I study weather:
fingertip, storm.

Can fire explain
this clang and racket?

Or am I the shudder,
my orchard come undone?

What a spill I've had!
What an education.

(I went as I was directed, a traveler *without path or guide, through a wilderness unknown:* vast interior me. Sometimes I meet *with favor and sometimes with nothing but frowns.)*

The Method

I use a little brush.
I rough me up:

all my tangles carded,
the wool of me undone.

Then the spinning.
Then the yarn

and lies: the thicket
of my face, trick

of the mirror's black
mood. Or the pond's,

ice gone white.
But how cold, the tin

of it, the lip at my lip.
Should I drink?

Should I weep
over geese, two by two?

Such love! And crumbs
can make them happy!

What treasure the feather
cast off: my fondest wish

come true: my *me*
at last, this plumage.

Nature Exhibit

In the Museum of Drawers,
of Birds' Bodies and 1901,
discretion is everything:
cotton in the mouth and cotton in the eyes.

Here, we embarrass easily,
as though we too are tagged
to silence, cannot resist the beauty of capture:
wings folded, elegant as fans
and that useless, necks arching back.

I read the flourish
of their names, elaborate penmanship,
record of when and where.

You imitate their sounds, their hollows
resonant and stunning.

What we don't voice is the luck
of their keeping, the portion we'd give
or want of such attention.

The Chimney

Forget birds, rain in winter.
Forget their lungs, throbbing.
Forget the shape of smoke.

This is not that chimney.

What flies here is your face;
what cries out, your hands.

Forget the house, the garden gate;
everything white or shuttered.

Forget your large name.

The sky dilates: a blue wider
than your mouth; an ache;
a mirror; a net.

Where are the sticks for rubbing?
Where is the flame in your palms?

The air quickens to black.

What falls is ashen
and familiar: your priceless legs,
your ruined waist.

The Mesmerist

Enough to watch one gloved hand, white
and the echo of white, like bells bells.

But where is the steeple, the tiny panes
of stained glass? Where are the ropes

for swinging, the willows beneath
a blue and certain sky? And explain

the innuendo of his fingertips, electric
above a face he almost strokes, a body

rocking back into the rasp of birdcalls,
into the woods beyond rows of pink stucco

houses, the safety of clotheslines and each
father's shirts waving *good-bye, good luck.*

What is this rough path, the panting and
gasp, gravel beneath these unlaced shoes?

Where's the whitewashed fence, the willing
garden? And whose voice and sudden touch

like slender light pleading with each leaf:
which veins are roads and how far back?

The Bereavement Room

I've left my fingertips on fence posts,
hooked my name from a tree,
a teacup in the branches.

I've dropped my numbered ribs
along the way, a path
back to where I pinned my heart

on a bush, reddest berry
any bird might pluck and swallow.
I've entered here, my skin

now pale wood hammered
with grief: my face a cabinet, eyes
on a shelf, lips in a jar.

Mockingbird Pie

Measure the slick of their voices,
what you'll smother with

                              your keen hands.

Take pleasure in the heft of them,

                                     in tin,
locked and cool in the pie safe.

Enough of their all-night riddling:
the way they cry

                covet covet
and think they're you.

A Short History of Anxiety

Consider dresses: the shapes
and the shapes beneath—

As in,
How can this one not fit?
And,
How can this other one also not fit?

⚜

Apple, pear, pencil, stick:

You've been to the fruit market,
the five-and-dime,
the lumberyard:

nothing looks good today.

⚜

Including The Slip Dress,
which was designed

"to reveal the body in ways that were irreconcilable—"

(yes, I see that—)

Or The Baby Doll Dress,
which offers

"luxury of motion and seductiveness"

(No, not like your dolls,
though on the rack
it does seem possible
you'd be that happy:
walk and talk—)

⚘

Both of these dresses "emanate from the shift."

 (What shift?)

   (You know, The Shift:
     as in definitions 2, 7b, and 8a and b,

   which include: a change
     of direction or form; a woman's

   undergarment; slip or
     chemise; a means to

   an end; expedient; a stratagem;
     trick—)

(Oh, *that* shift—)

⚘

So do you see now why your mother
whisked you through the department store,
didn't want you with her in the dressing room?

    (—that cubicle of unforgiving light)

Do you see why you've grown up this way?

⚘

But aren't they lovely,
tagged and hung?

    (Perhaps you think
    you could be this lovely—)

꩜

Even the vocabulary is dazzling:

> For example,
> > *architectonic* and *corset*,

> which are sort of the same thing,
> > or so historians tell us

> in discussions of the fashioning
> > of body shape, the inner layers

> and "the peel,"
> > which sounds vaguely—

꩜

But thank goodness
that's all done!
No day, tea, semi-
evening, or evening
dress for lucky you!

> > > (Though don't you love
> > > all that work: ribbons
> > > and lace, embroidery circa
> > > 1903, circa 1916, 1938?)

(Don't you sometimes wish?)

꩜

Given all this lack
> of—is it shelter?—

where you can hide
      your many and various

flaws, each one
      catalogued bad to worse,

                  is it any wonder?

🌿

Stratagem has two definitions:

    1. A military maneuver designed to surprise an enemy

        and

    2. A deception

from a root meaning, "to be a general"—

            So, which dress do you like?

🌿

Expedient is both an adjective and a noun

    meaning,
        Appropriate to a particular purpose—

    meaning,
        A contrivance adopted to meet an urgent need—

          So, what is your particular purpose?
          What is your urgent need?

Third Remove

Attic attic.
Every room is a high perch:

bell tower, bird feeder.
I ring and coo to no avail.

Why can't I throw me down,
blaze of something brilliant?

Why are there no telescopes
pointed my way?

(Remember: *I once had tender parents.* But who will dote on me
now, whose hands through my hair? *Down among the wild beasts,*
there is no applause, no good reason.)

The Bitter End

Bird, if you start now,
you'll not stop.
Can you imagine the forsythia?

Try. It is a boat.
It will rock you to sleep
if you want.

Silence can be company,
sometimes. Maybe
you could think of snow this way?

You've grown that white,
examine yourself in the mirror:
error error.

There's no use
in longing:
your breath on the window

is thin ice.
It will not hold you,
your eights, the age

you stopped believing
a name could be a rope.
Water, water—

the tub overflows.
Your plate overflows.
Can you imagine the spiral

of your body? Smaller,
it is the crumb
you reject,

what the drainpipe knows.
Can you imagine
your throat opening?

It wants
a tantrum. It wants
to make yellow happen.

After Arguing

Lavender snow, night tilts beyond
touch, the whiter house and sky.

Breathing goes filigree and quieter,
and I put my hands in their box,

hang my arms in ice and branches.
The streetlight sharpens, and you take

the salt I've kept in the cupboard,
all the wings I've hidden in the lake.

Raised in the Dark

What wood can do—what curves!
I mistook the table leg
for my mother's face, never questioned
such handless love. Until I learned,
I thought the clock's jagged beak
was my father's quick peck:
a bird alert to me
each quarter hour. I was proud
to bruise and know,
split my lip on pointed edges.
My body now a map of where I've been,
I think a drawer is fine:
folded just so,
I'm creased and happy:
I like the feel of wood beneath me,
I like to think I've come this far.

The Sorceress

Where are my affections,
in what box or hollow organ,
dirt or heart or lung?

My eyes darken
and go out, like evening.

I wish to stop
this diffusion: bits of me—
hair and ribbon—
catching on the hawthorn tree.

What debt requires
such payment? I give me
as *sky,* I give
me *dazzling* and *fragile.*

Now I'm a paper lantern,
ribs jutting, illuminated.
Now I'm a dull myth.

Display Case

I am small but not precious,
set down without language,
roped off.

Egg cup, remember me?
I'm the one who tapped my finger,
asked the glass, is this *in* or *out*?

Enough

Holding nothing, your stomach
is a jeweled purse. *Glitter,*
its sound, its beautiful anger.

You thin, you halve.

Your fingertips delight
in the white tablecloth, the luck
of crumbs. Mouth,

what a bad fish you are:
always begging *me me.*
Scold yourself.

The wrist does not complain.

See how she loves the mirror: herself,
the music of her bones,
their *chalk chalk.*

Isn't this everything
you've ever wanted?
Glimmer and wait.

Sequin, you grow exquisite.

"Feminism, The Body, and The Machine"

Scrap of paper, little pencil:
I am at the library.

I am searching
                    for a limb to go out on—

some little thing that will help me

                                write more than a torso—

(that old lyric problem—)

✤

This is a Process,
like sculpture, which I have read about,

the chisel,
the thrill and danger
                    (one wrong move and—)

✤

Or like collage.
From the French, from the Greek,
meaning, *to glue.*

Which sounds good.
As though anything can be made into something.

Such as this scrap of paper on which I write call numbers:

BF 1576.B6 *Salem Possessed: The Social Origins of Witchcraft*

and

BF 1566.W734 *Riding the Nightmare: Women and
        Witchcraft from the Old World to Colonial Salem*

꙼

So now I am a detective:

     Nancy Drew and the Case of the Missing Text.

Down on my hands and knees
I would like to know what life was like
for women in Colonial America.

So that I can write a poem.
Odd purpose.

Like Nancy finding the hidden jewels,
     then wearing them
though they do not belong to her—

꙼

But I have this scrap of paper,

    this scrap of text

       (cut, no doubt, by some librarian)

and I want to know

is it Feminism = The Body = The Machine?

     (which makes sense if you think of the body as a machine,
       i.e., out of your control,
             which I sometimes do—)

Or

is it Feminism vs. The Body vs. The Machine?

(which also makes sense
          since "versus" is how things feel

                              at least to me—)

Or what?

The questions seem to be:

      What is the intention of a comma?

      and

      How much can that small purse hold?

                    (See it? The one the sentence dangles
                              from her thin wrist—)

                    ✺

If I'm Nancy Drew

      (as I always wanted to be:
      crouching in the bushes at age 10,
      making notes on lined paper)

then I wouldn't carry a purse.
I'd carry a pocketbook,
                    which is like a purse, except not.

And I'd drop even that when I found the jewels—

          (string of pearls maybe—something respectable—)

because these feminine trappings
can interfere with my work.

Hence the difficulty for women in Colonial America.

Such as Anne Hutchinson,
        a.k.a. "This American Jezebel,"

who stirred things up

by "giving herself wholly
        to reading and writing."

To say nothing
of preaching the Gospel

                (which means "good tale,"
                    which sounds like a lie,
                which sounds like "goody,"
                    a woman of humble rank).

In short, these activities were "not fitting"
for her sex.

Also, she was a midwife.

End result: excommunication, banishment
        "as being a woman not fit for our society."

Which means, as a 20th-century historian tells us,

        she had no sense
                "of what was possible in this world."

⚘

Again, like sculpture.

> (one wrong move and —)

⚘

Or like punctuation.

> (one wrong comma and —)

> (—embarrassment—the contents of the

purse strewn everywhere—)

⚘

Which is why it's all so difficult—

> attaching the limbs,
> *finding* the limbs—

for this torso—
my torso.

Because Nancy never had one, not really.
She was all smarts.
She was not the whole thrill.

⚘

But Anne Hutchinson was.

Hence the threat.

After her excommunication, she suffered
    "a monstrous birth"

                    (or so writes John Winthrop, governor,
                        and foe of her kind—)

proof of witchcraft,
proof of something—

or so he confides in his diary:

        she gave birth to twenty-seven nothings,
            "altogether without form,"
        small as an "Indian bean,"
            large as "two male fists."

                        ❧

So are you implying he is The Machine?

                        (I don't know—)

Could *you* be The Machine?

                        (I don't know—)

                    ❧

This must be the limb I've gone out on.

                    (No, not Anne Hutchinson.)

This:

                    (See?)

This lyric:

(Do you understand now?)

This plunder:

Fourth Remove

I'm a good prisoner.
I keep my cup clean:

tin mirror, tin me.
I learn fast, master

preening, turn and turn,
until I wonder

what's the use of curtsy,
what's the thrill in ransom?

(Is it true that *the love for a disobedient child will increase, grow more ardent?* Surely, I am the test of this theory. Surely, nothing comes *to redeem or fetch me* now.)

Interview with Alice

How did you fall?
    I was wearing a blue pinafore.
    Which was the sky.
    No: which was not the sky.
    Never mind.

    Say: I was walking alone.

What did you think when you saw the key?
    I loved the key.

How small did you become?
    First: thimble, little bucket: fine.
    Then: smaller.
    Then: palpitation.
    Then: swept away.
    Then: good for nothing.

How large?
    Beyond keeping,
    my teeth—too much—
    my hair to brush—
    my arm ached.

Why did you come back?
    I tumbled up.
    I grew dull.

What will you be now?
        Correct, adequate, against my will.

Do you have any advice for other girls?
        I suppose.

Alice, Falling

i

What edges the world has!
What hidden grates
for a shiny coin like me
to just slip through—

ii

My starched dress, my blue sash:
I'm a pinwheel, and delightful.
I'm an optimist
and know to look for moss.
With my pointing finger raised,
I can find the wind's direction.

iii

Should I be hungry?
Should I think
of finger sandwiches, crustless bread?
Then the little cakes—
such sugar!—and guilt
my aching teeth confess.

iv

Am I so light?
Venturesome and rash?
Is my name a word somewhere still?
What landing can come of this
tumbling: my whole life
gone precarious—

v

My hair tangles and smells sweet.
I've lost my silver comb,
my engraved initials.
I'm beyond punishment.

Alice in the Hallway

I've got a golden key, and hands
white as milk, the big glass
I drink to make me strong.

So many lucky chances,
I hardly know what to wish:
each little door, a ribboned gift.

I need a funny hat. I need
balloon animals: a monkey
for company, a giraffe's silly neck.

Down on my knees like bedtime,
this is no birthday party.
The locks have heard me beg

when all my tantrums failed.
It's *pretty please* for a glimpse.
It's *sugar on top* for those flowerbeds.

Cracked Alice

Baby tooth, I finger
the button on my glove.
All day it wiggles loose
and I taste blood.

They say I've had a spill.
They say I've landed
myself in bed.

My little window pouts:
the garden's a tease.

Restless, I travel the bruise
on my elbow: yellow road
through the forest blues
and greens. Darker
needles at my face.

I've not had a dream.
Nothing hides beneath the bed.

But this bee won't quit
my ear, buzzes
from vines and trellis
painted on my cup and saucer.

Oh, how can I pretend?

There's a lump in my throat
I've named *ache, sugar,*
new best friend.

Spoiled Alice

O pout!
O fuss and bother!

He likes me a little
hurt, my small
invisible crown off-
kilter, my pretend
upset, upset.

What do I want
for his thumb in my mouth?
Dare I admit my tooth's
sweet for that comfort?

In his lap, I cross my arms
across my heart, pretend
I'm not wound
around his finger, a lock
of me, a pocket full of luck.

I've no patience
for his barnyard noises,
the hiss at my neck.
I do not arch or shiver.

Gothic Alice

I expect everything: bottomless
wells and empty buckets
or broken rope suggesting
God-knows-what. I must be
castle-bound, fated
for loose banisters and the endless
fall down staircases.
I bruise easily. I'm enamored
of the colors I turn.
Give me brooding
in the attic, my absent master,
and I want nothing more
than to oblige.
Hand me the poker
and I'll stoke the fire.
Tell me the wind has shifted
and I'll lean from his window,
let the shutters bang.

Femme Fatale Alice

Little noose, little loop
of cloth cut and the button's
free, fake pearl gleaming
between his teeth. I've learned
you never know: even my plain dress
can set him thinking, and pleats
are worse—the iron's edge thrills
and makes him jealous.
He says deep pockets imply
occupation: his hands
now a schoolboy's complaining
how cold. Strange
the way he likes my shoes,
begs to touch heels and laces,
my mosquito-bitten ankles.
Who knew he'd call my name
this way, whisper
I was the slip-and-fall
rabbit hole waiting to happen?

Thoroughly Modern Alice

I've shed my petticoats, I've unbuckled
my Mary Janes. Jagged mirror, jagged
me: my reflection grows Cubist:
skewed cheeks and rosy glow
dismantled. Were my hands
ever gloved, my voice
that cloying? Now I wish I'd read
my future in tea leaves, discovered
a name for this unrecognizable
girl, this defunct Alice.

Alice Writes Her Memoirs

Begin with *taken,* meaning: distance,
meaning: the clean girl I was,
apron strings tied—rabbit ears!—
at the small of my untouched
back: before I learned wind,
before the slip and impractical
patent leather I regretted—
pinched toes and tears enough
to fill the well that had no bucket,
no pulley back to bedtime: mother
and eyelet: my face scrubbed
of all want, my fists tight in prayer.

Alice Writes a Letter

Dear Me—!

    —Where do I begin? And where do I leave off? Once
my little finger was the brink of me, before the globe and
illumination, before I dirtied the hem of my best dress—
whip stitch, whip stitch—over and under that far edge.

    Last night I dreamed my hand along the surface, the
world the way it was before I learned *up* and *down, error*
and delight. I woke to the morning's bewilderment, my
vacant mirror. Still there is no scar on my cheek, no
elegant proof of *x equals*—

    Tell me: how am I to get through another day of
lessons? I am not clever with letters. I cannot make
myself make the shape of broken promises: a consonant's
dry well, a vowel's fraying rope.

    Oh chain of paper dolls, my hands are bruised! I am all
aboard this engine, this body—come what may—

                         I am no longer one of you—

Fifth Remove

IN WHICH THERE IS A CHOICE

O sack of cash! O prayer!
Enough is so dull.

Forget my rope and blade,
my cutting loose.

Leave me be.
I think *kept* a lovely word

and full of birds. How rare
their blue excess!

(*Before I knew what affliction meant,* I did not guess my hunger.
Insatiable, I rant: my portion's too small: suffering *hand to mouth.*)

The Disappearing Girl

What noise in her throat:
another trick must be trapped there,
a dove's complaints for air,
a little water please before the dark,
before his slender fingers
close each box, making magic.

Click click go the locks.
Tap tap goes his wand.

Gone her ponytail, the pink
ribbon he stroked and stroked.
Gone her cold hands, clasped.
Gone the bird that knew
her lungs, the blue-black air.

The little doors swing open,
then the velvet curtain.

He spins the box again and cries
her name, a spell to call
the coins he's placed, gold
perfume behind her ears.

The clapping's stopped, he's had
enough, he wants her now.

The Disappearing Girl's Mother Remembers

All knees and elbows, silly bird
restless at the table while I begged
just one more spoonful,
please, take another bite.

Weather vane at the roof's edge,
she turned for wind. I prayed
the house would hold her, the pink
gingham bed draw her back and down.

But her body gleamed like silver,
thin as the baton she loved, that
nimble, but who will catch her now,
my girl, thrown and twirling?

Her Sisters Agree

We called her *kite,* a bird of prey
she knew by heart,
the forked tail she drew
in books that spilled from the basket
on the bike she pedaled hard,
her scabbed knees eager for pavement
and crashing, her mouth
whistling for the sweet cut.

High in the tree we named
foolish pride, the one she called
lucky, she held
the white rope of her body
spellbound by leaves
crackling out instructions,
then wild applause

until he caught her,
offered her
words like *spotlight* and *sequins.*
She touched the dark rim
of his hat, his rough face.
He smoothed her hair
and hushed the little songs
we longed to believe
were protests.

The Magician as a Boy

Good with his hands and fond
of edges, he collected bottle caps
that cut his palms, and speckled stones
he'd lick to shining, then polish
full speed in his rock tumbler.
Once he freed a feather, blue
and caught in prickly shrubs.
He held it to his lips: a little thrill
to wonder if the bird flew lopsided
or was lame and had bled,
would want him now tender.

The Disappearing Girl's Homemade Magic Show

Mirror, mirror, am I silk
enough to be a scarf,
or should I grow feathers,
squawk or coo?

I need a hiding place:
tree branch or dresser drawer.
I need a hand to pull me from
the well of a black hat.

Look! there's fluttering
in my wrist: bird's pulse: no,
highwire and rope ladder
I'll climb to the drum roll,

spotlight on the gaping
mouths afraid I'll unravel
and not stop: all threads,
begging as I go: *silence, please.*

His Bag of Tricks

Beyond the playing cards'
bent edges, beyond

the scarves, each silk
blindfold, he keeps her

gloves and lipstick,
a few strands of hair

caught in the pink
ribbon he stole

and holds close to his lips
as though to taste the girl

he's almost got now,
his white rabbit.

The Magician Explains How

Think of corsages saved.
Think of folding laundry.
Think of her sweet limbs,
the gentle crushing.

Careful of spotlights,
careful of the clock.
Careful of your hands shaking
the darkness in her eyes.

Remember the words back,
remember to smile,
remember her lovely neck
and where you put her.

The Disappearing Girl Explains

Not so dark back here: voices
know my name, their hands
braid my hair to silk.
Should I care who they are?

He wound my heart into a clock,
but I learned to swallow feathers,
designed a bird to tell me when
to whistle for distraction.

I've got a little trick: sequins
counted to forget, my spangled
bodice sparking, and the throat
he likes to touch.

The good dark never lasts:
all the voices tangle into his,
a rattling at the cage and me
clutching my pretty bird.

Private Showing

I lock his hat in its tall box.
I knot his scarves:
each one a bright fist.

I leave my lipstick
and hairbrush on the dresser,
my fake diamond earrings.

All around us, caged birds
mill and peck, ring their bell.
The white rabbit cleans his fur.

I imagine their simple hearts
like empty coin purses,
jealous and clasping.

On the windowsill, he keeps
stones I'll hold in my mouth
then give to him, shining.

The Disappearing Girl Returns Home

There's the tree I dared to drop me.
There's my body, and the dumb sky

I invented. I envied birds' nests,
the way they made something from nothing:

weaving twigs and spit and hair.
Inside the house, the pink gingham bed

where my mother smoothed the tiny wings
jutting from my back. As though

to encourage sleep. As though flight
was not my obsession: sleek

disappearance. Did the neighbors know
I was such trouble: bruised

and fascinated? Did they watch
as I pounded my fists against the black

box of the tree, tumbling through branches,
practicing my graceful exit?

Sixth Remove

IN WHICH THERE IS CONCLUSION

Listen, Providence:
deliver me

more of this prize,
delay my restoration.

(Are there wounds? I cannot say —)

Devilkin

My dolls lock themselves in their house
and refuse all but a man's rough touch.

He is a god to them.
He is a bear: growl and warm.

I break in, give them stigmata,
bandage each plastic wrist.

They keep perpetual adoration.
They are consumed.

I gather cups and spoons, say
I will catch the blood!

They blink—blue eyes, sweep of lashes—
they think me *excessive.*

What they love is *lair,* the word where he sleeps,
his clumsy hands curled about his head.

Devil and the Deep Blue Sea

What a dinghy I am! Oarless
and nearly wishing *waterfall*
for a reason to be careless
come what may. I cannot
worry anymore or say my prayers.
A leaf falls yellow into my lap.
Tulip tree, it is an odd corsage.
I am hardly anyone's *most likely*
unless it's *sink or swim.*
Another penny tossed up, it might
fit into my loafers but won't
help me call home. The house
is empty anyway, just an old sheet
and sofa cushions. I made it myself.
I have the rug burns to prove it.
Down on my knees, you'd think
I have religion, scrap of cloth,
holy shroud tucked in my wallet.
It cannot pay the bills or buy a dress
sequined and reckless as the sky,
night where my dolls keep house.
They come with such little brooms
and dustpans, such good intentions.
But what drudgery! They beg
for bedtime stories, white pillows.
I rub their aching backs and whisper
I was a doll once too! I remember
the high shelf, the dust in my hair.
I remember the hands at my throat.
But that's all done. Now I'm a boat,
a black eye bobbing in the tub.
I know there's a drain. I know
bubbles can't conceal everything
that's wrong with me. I admit
I had to steal that leaf for company:
the *ouch!* was mine and not the tree's.

Gretel: A Case Study

i
I'm all right in a small space.
As long as I can turn around,
I'm fine inside myself—

ii
I miss the little feather bed,
                    which was mine,

and the white coverlet,
                    which was also mine.

iii
First I said *please*.
Then I said *thank you*.

iv
We had wandered
and came upon a little wish—
hint of peppermint,
hint of
            —oh, I can't remember what—

But later, an ache
and we regretted—

v
The trees were not the trees we knew.
The sky was not the sky.
Birds cried *cru-el, cru-el,*
and pebbles talked amongst themselves.

vi
When I saw the oven,
I clapped my hands together.

vii
Hansel is not the animal.
I am the animal.
I carry my own low growl.

Listen: can you hear it?

No, not that.

Listen harder:

One Thing or Another

Behind the sky: another, bluer.

Inside these winter trees:
leaf song and bird song,
their tender, arching throats.

Beyond your face: a lake,
waterglass, my smooth hand.

And deeper: fish: delicate
fins, wind in gills, and hook
scars, musical in water.

The Parts of a Flower

A small village:
to market, to market,
skipping all the way,
dust on my patent leathers,
pollen in my hair.

Hold my hand
into the factory of buttons,
all pink; into the room
of blown green glass, hot
and turning; into the forge,
the blacksmith's black
hammer pounding.

This is the pistil
and these are the stamens.
Notice how delicately they
rise, slender. And discrete:
the envelope of petals
a secret ballot
the bees will count.

They are just mouths,
wild talk and honey
I'll wear at my ears,
sweet to taste.

The tip of your tongue
gives you away:
the smooth of another peddler.

Your coat opened wide,
you hawk everything
essential: saplings and shiny
trowels, a corsage to match
the light in my eyes,
the tiny pinup sun.

Planetarium

Gibbous moon, night clicks:
a locket's tiny picture: constellation
of *my hand at your mouth.*
Or another sky and quiet I opened:
the drawer of birds, cotton beneath
their stunned and brilliant bodies.
Folded down, they're exotic
as the hairpin washer I admired—
color of dusk—small token you'd offer
if this were Japan, 17th century,
my hair at last come loose.

Bright Waiting

Birds return early, hunger
and cries in the maze
of arborvitae: clamor
you understand. Hands
rush and settle. Rush.
String your breath along:
bead, bead. Your skin
shimmers like dusk,
like wings and runoff.
All night you clock the sky.
You crocus beneath it,
you ribbon and tendril.

Dash

Consider *dash,* to break
     or smash by striking
violently, and *dash,*
     a sudden movement
or quick stroke,
     a rush, Morse code,
a foot race—

               (Consider yourself—)

                ✺

Consider Emily Dickinson,
whose dash did not fit,
was "normalized"—

               (Have you ever
               been "normalized"?
               How might that
               hurt?)

                ✺

So what was her dash
if it was not a footrace?
               (oh, it was a footrace)

O.K., what about
Morse code, a rush?
               (oh, it was a rush and code)

O.K., then
what is the problem here?

The problem is I don't know
what to make of the dash.

For example, is it a blade
or a paper cut?

Where does the hurt
come from?

And how did Dickinson intend—

(How do I—)

The other problem was her
dash could be too spirited,
too Morse code, too much—

And this includes her poems.

(But now everything's easier.
Haven't you found that
to be true?
Hasn't your experience been—)

Like that. That dash.

Which means

I cannot answer that question

or

Here is my answer and here is my other answer

Which is why Dickinson struggled—

                              (Which is why I—)

                              ✺

Surely you have felt like this:

        all your hopes dashed—
                by—what was it?—

        the weight of convention?
                But don't forget

        what you've gained:
                remember? distance—

        Oh yes! that convenient other
                dash that keeps you

        at arm's length—

                              ✺

Another problem is how the dash becomes
a mirror, the way you look at it and say

        my lips are sealed—

        or

        I lay me down—

The fear implicit
The crack of light

The threshold,
    which you cross—

The frontier,
    where bad things—

꙰

But isn't God in the dash?

       Well, yes, occasionally God has been known
          to reside there, to come around—

This is what makes it a frontier.

      (This is why—)

꙰

Do you get the feeling everything is a clue, including Dickinson,
who is not here by accident? Do you get the feeling a poem is a
record of the clues, with the dash as the *x marks the spot?*

꙰

So, what is the real problem,
    what is it at this spot?

And can you make a poem of it,
    dash one off?

As in, can you perform hastily,
    can you shatter—

(Yes! Look, here:
here are the pieces
of me—)

🌿

The dash says *I know you*—

The dash says
hurry up!

no,

wait—

Notes on Sources

Two of these poems owe a debt of gratitude to the following sources from which quotations were taken and in some cases adapted.

"A Short History of Anxiety": *Infra-Apparel* by Richard Martin and Harold Koda

" 'Feminism, The Body, and The Machine' ": The information about Anne Hutchinson came from a variety of sources, including *Salem Possessed: The Social Origins of Witchcraft* by Paul Boyer and Stephen Nissenbaum, *The Salem Witchcraft Trials* by Karen Zeinert, and *Riding the Nightmare: Women and Witchcraft from the Old World to Colonial Salem* by Selma R. Williams and Pamela Williams Adelman

THE OHIO STATE UNIVERSITY PRESS /
THE JOURNAL AWARD IN POETRY

David Citino, Poetry Editor

1998	Walt McDonald	*Blessings the Body Gave*
1997	Judith Hall	*Anatomy, Errata*
1996	John Haag	*Stones Don't Float: Poems Selected and New*
1995	Fatima Lim-Wilson	*Crossing the Snow Bridge*
1994	David Young	*Night Thoughts and Henry Vaughan*
1993	Bruce Beasley	*The Creation*
1992	Dionisio D. Martínez	*History as a Second Language*
1991	Teresa Cader	*Guests*
1990	Mary Cross	*Rooms, Which Were People*
1989	Albert Goldbarth	*Popular Culture*
1988	Sue Owen	*The Book of Winter*
1987	Robert Cording	*Life-list*

THE GEORGE ELLISTON POETRY PRIZE

1987	Walter McDonald	*The Flying Dutchman*
1986	David Weiss	*The Fourth Part of the World*
1985	David Bergman	*Cracking the Code*